When You See a Butterfly

Miranda Hughes

Copyright © 2024 Miranda Hughes
All rights reserved.
ISBN-13: 979-8-3240-4622-4

Dedication

Dedicated to my sweet girl in Heaven, my Blakely Ruth. She gave me the inspiration to write this story, because she visits me ever so frequently in the form of a Butterfly, inspiring me to write this beloved story to share with her brother and sister, her cousins, family, and friends. With hope, to all of you who need a reminder that your loved one you are missing is always closer than you think even when you can't see them. Blakely brought so much joy to others lives, her joy can continue to live on through me writing in her honor. Mommy loves you so much sissy. Let your wings soar.

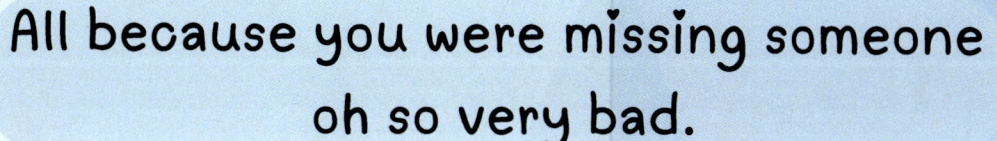
All because you were missing someone oh so very bad.

They are always there with us even though they can't be seen.

For our loved ones that we are missing so much,
will flutter on by in the most surprising way..

For its someone that your heart has been missing coming to see you each new day.

Your Butterfly friend would want you to know,
that they love YOU oh very so.
But, please don't be sad when your Butterfly leaves...

The End.

About the author

Miranda Hughes, born and raised in Tulsa, Oklahoma. She is a mom, wife, and newly published author.

She embarked on the journey of creating a fun and inviting children's book as a way to get her creative spark flowing and to honor her late daughter, Blakely Ruth.

As you read her first published book, When You See a Butterfly, you will understand the loving meaning of when you see a butterfly. Thank you for supporting a mom's dream, her biggest hope is that this book leaves you with a smile. As Miranda says, remember to be kind today.

Find this book on Amazon.com!

Remember to always be kind.

Made in the USA
Coppell, TX
25 January 2025